BIOG

Linda Larson is a story-teller and writer of this collection of poetry. She is also an artist and all of the paintings in the book are hers.

Linda overcame a childhood tragedy to now live more in the moment and find the coincidental gifts of the day. She has three college degrees, two wonderful sons, a daughter-in law, and enjoys living in the Midwest.

PREFACE

I wrote this book because I wanted people to know they are not alone in how and what they feel. All feelings are on the table.

I have slowly healed from a car accident that killed my sister, brought depression and sorrow to my parents, and gave me a deep sense of abandonment. I finally learned to put my feelings on paper. Writing gave me some objectivity and truth. Moving through sorrow, pain, and struggles, I have come home to myself. I have more of an openness that has led to more joy and intimacy with myself and others. Humor has played a big part in my healing. I hope you will connect with something I have written. Good to meet you!

ACKNOWLEDGMENTS

I first honor the great loving Spirit I call the Divine. The Spirit has guided me to share my art and words connecting me with others.

James Pressler, leader of the Writers' Group of Park Forest listened to my poems and kindly critiqued them. His insight and humor provided me courage in speaking my words.

Kim Olver, leader of the Writers' Group from the Professional Woman's Network, was an especially powerful influence. Kim set firm and kind goals for me so I would move from disbelief to embracing this new creative venture.

I want to thank Kristin Nieter whose clear thinking and preciseness gave me the focus I needed to move forward. She is a writer and has published a book of devotions in honor of her late grandmother.

Iris Blumenthal, an editor and fellow art student, agreed to review and edit my poetry. She was invaluable in correcting my spelling, punctuation, and content for clarity.

Kathy Hawn and Kadi Finlayson Meyer gave me honest, direct peer review I needed.

Donna Dukes, Kortni Springer, Michelle Borgman, and Mallory Blink are librarians and assistant librarians at the

Oak Forest Acorn Library. Their patience and information helped me learn about hard drives and computers, objects of much confusion at times.

My friends who heard and understood my poetry gave me a growing sense that I was on the right path. I cannot name them all for they are many.

CONTENTS

STRUGGLE AND CONFUSION

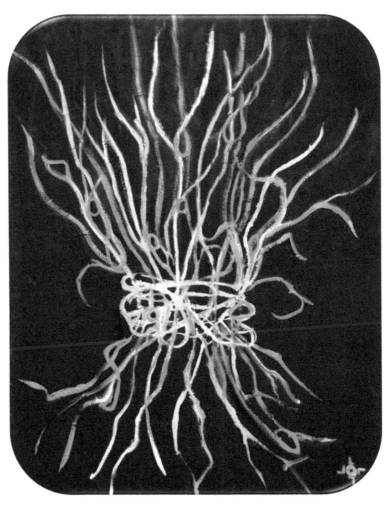

TANGLED

NAME

What I do not want is fame.

Just want someone to know my name.

Do I count to someone here?

Does anyone hold me dear?

Knowing me inside,

Loving me with pride.

Of all the people in the hall,

Do I matter then, at all?

Does it matter

That I came?

Does anyone here

Know my name?

SANE

In a world of pain, can I be sane?

Can I be free with others chained?

Fear and strife, a way of life?

Pain the way for every day?

Cool and breezy, nice and easy;

Others do. Me too?

Floating free, peace, calmness

Inside of me.

Not a startle reflex, but calm resolve

With a twinkle in my eyes.

ILLUSIONS

Illusions comfort me.

I need them rich and deep.

Don't tell me they aren't true.

Illusions I WILL keep.

SAFE?

I loved my own illusions.

They kept me safe and warm.

Living in a fantasy,

What could be the harm?

Because of many forces,

I let some fond dreams go.

It was excruciating,

With blood and bits to show.

I'm living in a strange world,

Halfway here, halfway there.

Trying to like the new,

I find it very bare.

FEAR

Fear

No, wait,

Big error.

Insidious,

Gut wrenching

Sharp-clawed terror.

UNCERTAINTY

I have to surrender

Those I cannot control.

The thought strikes my heart

To the core.

Ask for the Sun,

Ask for the Moon,

Do not want...

The room with no floor.

COOKING

I stew in my own juices,

Flavors bland and flat.

No moving or inspiration,

Just sat and sat and sat.

Want a stronger flavor,

Want spices to enlive,

Sparkling wine, spicy peppers.

I want joy, not just survive.

MIND

Don't need no enemy.

Got myself so fine.

Painful thoughts

Eat me from inside.

THE RISK

Up, up the ladder, high into the sky,

I reach the tiny platform with a deep, heavy sigh.

For I must catch the swinging bar,

Grasp it with sweaty palms,

And jump into the air.

What will happen? Will I fall?

Could it possibly be true

That in midair I could risk being new?

It is the bravest thing I've ever done to reach the other side,

For old attitudes from childhood have one by one just died.

HARD CONVERSATION

Never asked, did not belong.

Against my will

Came Peace and Calm.

"Peace and Calm, don't you stay.

Jump from a cliff...

That's my way."

Peace and Calm boldly said,

"We're here to stay;

You've been misled."

Did not resist, stood my ground,

Opened my arms.

I had been found!

WRITING

Confusion inspired,

Also pain,

I began writing

To keep me sane.

Will writing cease?

It's what I fear.

When joy bursts out,

And puzzles disappear?

BLANK

Sometimes I get crazy.

Try a thing or two.

Shoot for the moon?

Fly a balloon?

Ideas right now…

Too few!

DAYS

Some days

I retreat

Back into bed,

Hide my head,

Avoid the dread

Of what's...

Outside.

MORNING

Thank heaven for mornings.

I have hope with the day.

Get out dark cobwebs!

Racing mind, stay away!

FREEZE

Played a game of "freeze."
Wasn't a game at all.
Saved my sanity,
Though I curled up like a ball.

Could not feel most feelings
So I could exist.
Got through the terror
Of a family blown to bits.

Time to continue thawing,
For my mind, it's a must.
I'll take baby steps
Leading to self-trust.

There is no shortcut for the steps
If I do stand tall.
It is because I struggled hard,
Many times did fall.

May I have compassion
As I learn to think and choose.
Make decisions for each day,
As old ideas I lose.

THE DRAGON

Blood splattered, ripped flesh,

Still they would fight on.

She was cornered, bathed in sweat,

As the dragon sang a killing song.

She drew her sword named "Risk and Dare,"

Thrust it hard into the air.

The Dragon ignored the sword on high,

But steel pierced its single eye.

Both screamed in pain.

They were in many ways one.

The dragon slowly shrank,

His death had finally come.

ANGER

Anger is forbidden.

Told myself not to fight.

But I became divided;

Each of me took flight.

Anger is human,

Part of the Spirit's plan.

To feel, to reveal

Each woman, each man.

I am awkward being honest.

Don't know how I feel.

I struggle to be genuine,

United as one, and real.

MONSTERS

In the darkness of the night,

When I am alone with fright,

All the monsters come to jeer.

I feel helpless, consumed by fear.

What fault or deed I've done?

Who does not love me? Life without fun?

Some mistakes brought to light.

These, the demons of the night.

INERTIA

Here comes old inertia.

It slithers slow but sure.

Wanting to seize its prey,

Devour me, for sure.

REAL

Falling down to the ground

For real and in my mind.

I was dazed, bruised, in pain.

Shock...

Was truly mine.

P I T

Pit of despair,

Sounds so trite

Until...

YOU are there.

F L O W

Like things neat and tidy,

Life's a mess at best.

Back and forth it flows,

No stopping...

For a moment's rest.

N E W

New normal feels so odd.

Parts don't fit like they should.

I can't balance,

Feet don't work

Stand upright...

If I could.

LET GO

Hard to let adventures go,

They were exciting, real.

They are over, I am sad.

Want again to feel.

The noise and touch of them,

Love, growth did teach.

This moment is all I have.

It is within my reach.

CHANGE

Pondering has its place.

Need to use my brain.

Get up, and take some action.

Do NOT be the same.

FLOWING

It's wise to know the movement:

Start,

Middle,

End.

I see ends becoming:

Beginnings,

Over,

Again.

PROBLEMS

Decided to call problems

"Life lessons," very real.

Surprised when I changed the words,

I had joy to feel.

UNCERTAINTY

Uncertainty can be good?

Would believe it if I could.

Vomit, gag, spit I must.

It's rock-hard safety

For which I lust.

AWKWARD

Opposites together

Messily I go.

Left foot there,

Right foot stays,

Not an even flow.

Will this always be?

Want to glide with ease.

Damn and shit

I don't fit,

In this humanity.

OIL PAINTINGS

Happy with friends

Things going well.

Why do my paintings

Look like hell?

An homage to Havana,

More abstract than clear.

Another has pale colors,

Going nowhere, I fear.

These are my children.

I want them to shine.

Right now, I confess;

Don't say they are mine.

PAIN

Pain — it sucks, tell you true,

Want it out right now.

Tried to run to stop the pain,

At first not knowing how.

Should I respect the pain?

It hurt in my sleep.

It got me out of victimhood,

A torturous climb so steep.

MY HEART

That terrible exploding sound

Was a family lost, not yet found.

Tried to put my torn heart back

With magic that I lacked.

Giving up hopes and dreams

With tape and twine, I made a seam.

Sewing reality, the pieces meet.

Not the same, but my heart can beat.

CHOICE

Change is not bad; it's called "growing up."

Can't say I am surprised.

Eye to eye challenges, very strong;

Me, growing before my eyes.

Want others to play the game,

To decide where to move.

Thrill and fear in taking risks.

Each step, I now choose.

WAITING

Waiting is something

Not just empty space.

Want to accept it,

With much better grace.

ASSUMPTIONS

Assumptions,

Hard and strong,

Carved in stone,

Often...

Wrong.

INTERNAL STRUGGLE

Tug of war, grasping a rope.

Sweat and resistance to see.

Let the rope go.

Let life flow.

Dope on the rope,

Often me.

SAFE

Deep in food to give me care,

Want mac-and-cheese so smooth.

Music going to my heart,

As I seek to soothe.

Truth can be quick,

It can be clear.

It's just that I don't

Want to hear.

STRUGGLE

Moving with uncertainty,

Is a rugged place.

No place to cling,

Feet want to stop.

I am way, way off base.

ZOMBIE

Have you ever seen a zombie,

Legs stiff, eyes staring straight ahead?

Today I was a zombie,

As I got up from my bed.

Trying to reach the kitchen,

Making coffee just for me.

Water, filter, please don't spill.

My goal... just to be.

CREAM OF WHEAT

This day is like cream of wheat

Boring, bland, and dull.

No amount of sugar

Could energize my skull.

It's temporary I do know.

A time will come to risk.

Clocks moving slowly now,

Put in a movie disk.

DENIAL

Fear led to denial

Where I was safe and warm.

Stayed too long, denial strong,

Did to me much harm.

DRAINS

I am judging others

Compassion I should have sought.

Writing these words on paper

Drains poison from my heart.

REST

Why do I fear death?

Don't I need a rest?

I've had struggles

Also joy with zest.

Who could go on forever?

I'd like an afternoon nap.

Lived faithful with no regrets,

Lay my head on earth's soft lap.

LIES

Lies and truth in battle.

Science and opinions clash.

Act in wisdom, act in care

Before we turn to ash.

TRIBES I

Tribes were useful long ago

Protecting groups of folk.

Tribes can split us far apart,

Their tight bindings choke.

TRIBES II

It is an accident I live well fed

When deserving others starve.

What tribe is mine over time?

A one world view must carve.

REFLECTION

Waiting leads somewhere.

Quiet strains our ears

To hear directions for living

Making the next step clear.

This time of reflection

Can give a painful gift.

Dross is drained away,

What is real, will lift.

PAST

The past does not define me.

This moment is the one.

A gift of what is real...

Struggle and also fun.

LOVE AND LOSS

ALMOST TOGETHER

NO FLOOR

Into the room with no floor,

I want to say... nevermore.

But again and again I'm brought

To the threshold I have not sought.

To risk, to dare, to trust anew,

Power Almighty, the Holy You.

BOOK CLUB SISTERS

We each came spinning from our spheres
Unsure of what would be.
Slightly stiff, how would we fit
In this new tapestry?

Slowly growing, reaching out,
Sharing food so good.
We celebrate each other,
Delighted that we could.

Telling of pain and of joy
Became our important task.
No one criticized but offered support.
What more could we ask?

Time together, speaking truth
We each embraced the call.
Weaving together our common thread
Made us sisters after all.

MY MAN

Loved a man,
Slowly began to believe.
He goes to church on New Year's Eve.

We argued on Christmas,
Words very strong.
Both said, "You are wrong."

I love this man.
Our feelings out front.
Found we could both be blunt.

Don't know the future.
He said, "Stay with me,
The best is yet to be."

I hold in my heart, at this time
A delightful man…
Temporarily mine.

SO LOVED

Feel so loved, would you believe?

My heart used to have a hole.

Where was the piece to fill it up?

Had it once been sold?

The wreck tore my heart;

Seemed broken beyond repair.

Forces strong, held me in its arms.

Love gave to me a spare.

DESIRE

He's not the one

This I know.

Then why do I

Desire him so?

WHOLE STORY

Hello, goodbye

But I have seen

Much joy

In between.

FISHING

Who caught whom?

Hard to say.

The catch delicious

Either way.

PIECE

A puzzle piece came to fit

Into my jumbled life.

Been yearning for this piece;

It caused me much strife.

More complete, I live

Grateful for this gift.

Irregular shapes join...

In one amazing fit.

UNIT

You are.

I am.

What I see

United together...

Are

We.

HARD

Why is it so hard

To let love in my heart?

Believing love a trick,

Doubting from the start.

Wanting to believe

So I could receive

Another person...

Who fits me like a sleeve.

STAY

Who came and did not go?

Who stayed to love me so?

I am surprised, amazed, honored though,

By who came and did not go.

LOVE

Your love slips into cracks

When I am unaware.

Entering the smallest place

Exposing my heart bare.

GOLD

What you gave.

What you told.

What I received

Equaled gold.

Do not fear it stolen.

In my heart it stays.

I can take it out at will,

Precious in my gaze.

THE GIFT

You tied balloons

To a tree.

Hung a swing of rope and wood

In its shade...

Now I be.

TEASING

Love to tease the one I love.

Often wondered why.

Intimacy, joy, truth

In teasing's message lie.

E-MAIL

I savor the words you send,

Full of kindness, wisdom, wit.

Deeper we reach each other,

Joining spirits as we sit.

REUNION

We met, then went separate ways.

Countries we did roam.

Together now, I am more wise.

Have found my way back home.

THE WAY

A wounded man

Came my way.

He had sparkles on.

We did get close

In fits and starts.

But then, he was gone.

I'll miss his words, his laughter, touch.

I find myself

Missing him much.

TRUST

Wonder if I'll know next time

Whom I can trust for real.

Learned I deserve the best,

That is what I feel.

NO CAMELOT

Been living in a fairy tale.

Emotions high,

Many sighs,

Then it all went stale.

Camelot died.

Hopes were smashed,

People clashed,

And to myself I lied.

W H E E E E E

Looking for passion, had it once.

Loved the excitement it brought.

Ordinary is dull, numbing my skull.

Want passion again to start.

GUILT

Guilt did not work,

Pleading as a friend.

If I gave him money,

It would never end.

Recovery from wounds

Too deep for him to see.

He must do it for himself.

Rescuer, not me.

TRUTH

Nothing like a word of truth

To cut through dreams of bliss.

He could have died of drunkenness

And he'd be greatly missed.

Don't give a damn if he dislikes it.

What friend would I be

If I laughed and passed it off?

His death, don't let me see.

PAIN

It hurts to be misunderstood

When wanting to connect.

The power only lies with me

In what I can project.

The other person speaks for self.

I cannot speak for him.

Must let go of both of us.

No message can I send.

DIVORCE ?

Should I leave? Should I stay?

Will it be another day?

Change my life, not turn back.

Never step upon a crack.

Step by step so small to see,

I will do what works for me.

Leave the old, be the new.

To myself I will be true.

DECEPTION

No spies involved.

No cloak to hide.

Just words untrue,

Said side by side.

Toxic words

Spread us apart.

The game was over,

From the start.

GREY IN THE DARK

Ugly words,

Bones left bare.

Woman derided;

I was there.

I'm not a cat.

It is not dark.

Said as a joke.

Words cut a mark.

THE SIGN

"Please degrade me,"

There was a sign

Written on my face.

Walk in, stay a while, now go debase.

Shocked to see myself

So lacking in self-care.

Later writing words of truth,

Laid myself quite bare.

HIM

A wounded heart

Thought he was smart.

Used and deceived with ease.

He was proud,

Laughed out loud.

Did just what he pleased.

BEING IN LOVE

Want to be in love.

Clasp and hold them tight.

Did I say, "Them?"

Oh my, more than one,

A puzzle and delight.

STARS

Being in love

Opened me wide.

I twinkled in and outside.

Now dull events

With meager light,

Do not shine or bring delight.

BOUNDARIES

Boundaries set;

Tore them from my heart.

Shocked and sad,

Gave up some lies.

Still reeling from the smart.

GOOD / BAD

How could something be so good

And still turn out so bad?

Thought I had it all complete;

He's gone now, I am sad.

Not just sad, but wiser, too.

Now I've power to see

A world more realistic.

Guess what? Even me.

EVENING

Writing e-mails,

Speaking truth,

Like we're sitting close.

Sipping sherry,

Silence easy,

Loving this time the most.

MOTHER

Mother, head thrown back,
Laughing loud with glee.
Making deep plum pies,
Hot and fragrant for me.

You told tales of bravery
While feeling a great lack.
You left a town in Kansas
While never looking back.

You could change your mind,
When I did protest.
You wanted my own good.
You sought my very best.

Lover of beauty,
We liked pictures on the wall.
Chose the Flemish masters
As most beautiful of all.

Scarred in face and heart
By the accident in the car.
Our family forever changed,
Your mind then went afar.

Bearer of heartbreak
For two children lost.
You moved ahead, slowly.
This life had its cost.

Thank you for the gift of you,
Despite our clash of wills.
Your arms enfolded me with warmth
And also loved me still.

GIFT

Some presents have ribbons

Some, colors bright.

Wrapping to tempt,

Delightful in my sight.

The gift I treasure most,

Where do I begin?

One special gift came wrapped

In delicious, warm, brown skin.

STRENGTH

What makes someone valuable?

Not wealth, status, or such.

I must hold in my hand

The sturdy rock of trust.

Honor to stand when battered

Against storms, danger, and pain.

Able to rise, stand upright,

There quietly remain.

LOVED HIM

I loved him so

From head to toe.

Our passion did run deep.

We could not cross

The differences

That were so very steep.

We had a home

With two fine sons.

Music was in the air.

I signed the papers

But still have love,

If I'm really fair.

Y O U

Thought a man had a heart.

Thought him wise and smart.

Found inside an empty man.

Saw just grains of sand.

THE PRICE

I cannot pay the price you asked:

Not to speak, or feel, or think.

For in accepting your "niceness,"

I began to shrink.

Gave up my voice

Saying what was true.

Gave away my power, rights,

To another person — you.

Reclaiming what is mine,

It is time for me to go.

Took a lifetime of work,

Going very slow.

DIVORCE

All my emotions and brain,
Strained to finish the task.
Papers signed, terse words said,
With a business-like mask.

I've held myself in check,
To counter overload.
At last could move ahead
Along this painful road.

Once over, people said,
"Now you must feel relieved."
But I found other emotions,
Deep inside of me.

Anger and fear were these
As I went through motions of work.
Wondering how I could give and care,
For responsibility, I could not shirk.

Take time to calm, time to cry,
Time for it all to sink in,
Not in moments but in days,
So I could begin again.

FAMILY

What makes some people family?

Birth, spirit, or what?

Do hearts meet or words go forth,

The empty air to cut?

Do I know these people,

Talking, laughing, there?

Do they know me, as I am?

Do they really care?

It is a relief to meet again

For only a moment in time.

Our history goes back a while,

A history truly mine.

HOLIDAYS

I am not a token

To show at holidays.

To make you feel more normal

Or ease your guilt some ways.

I am alive and searching

Wanting to share who I am.

Will you reach out and hear me?

And listen if you can?

Or will there be distance?

Each going our own way?

Meeting like strangers

At the holiday.

CAROL ANN

Your life was brief.

You meant so much.

But I do not remember you.

My parents grieved so deep

For a beautiful child

They could not keep.

REMEMBER

I just remembered

I belong where all are welcome,

Where unexpected visitors enter my cocoon,

Where saying, "namaste" is real,

Where taking turns is normal,

Where people hug, lifting my feet off the floor,

Where people are possibilities, not the "other,"

Where art ignites mine.

So glad I remembered,

Because... I had forgotten.

LUST

I may look normal.

I'm filled with desire.

Do my daily tasks

Feeling on fire.

To lust this way

Is out of synch.

At times

It brings me to the brink.

Of what?

I do not know.

Only time and living

Will tell me so.

I KNOW

I know you like the things I do

Like shop and clean and cook.

I know you think you know me

As a person knows a book.

I want to be loved for who I am

Reaching to be free.

I want to be seen, heard, and cherished

For the spirit that lives in me.

HEALING

Grateful for healing in my family;

It's taken a long, long time.

Thought it would not happen;

Found closeness in those called mine.

Grateful for the Spirit's plan;

Desiring all things whole.

Working in unknown ways;

Transforming our very souls.

U S

Thought my marriage a mistake,

Just a short-term view.

Now I see more clearly,

Marriage a step for two.

Found so many barriers,

Mainly right in me.

I blamed most on others.

I could not really see.

Learned what not to do,

To imprison another close.

Learned respect is important,

With self-care, the most.

STUCK

Wouldn't it be ironic

If out of this terrible muck,

We learned to change,

Learned to care,

And loving really stuck?

MISERY

I'm causing my own misery.

Surrender him if I'm smart.

I sit on the edge, feet dangling,

So is my own heart.

KIND

Speak words of care

When keys are lost,

When tempers flare.

We are imperfect,

Mistakes often small.

We are creation's gift

On this round ball.

AUTHENTICITY

TREE OF LIFE

AUTHENTICITY

Been many places.
Wanted out of my skin.
Seeking authenticity,
Not knowing it came within.

Looked many places.
Thought others knew the way.
Found within myself,
A place I was to stay.

Confronted demons,
Fought fears so deep.
Took baby steps
Even in my sleep.

Had to heal broken parts.
Thought they would destroy.
Found the steep journey,
Leading me to joy.

THE PRIZE

Thought I had been cursed.
Doomed to a life of pain.
The wreck destroyed our family,
One seemed to go insane.

A child taking care of mother
At the age of 5,
Never able, always trying,
Just to keep alive.

The heavy load of "ought's,"
Pushed down below my heart;
Made living often leaded,
Oh, it was quite an art.

Seeking safety behind others,
In shadows of their might.
I only hoped to delay,
The terror of my fright.

Something slowly happened,
Changed my life profound.
Healing forces growing
In and all around.

My jealously of others,
Slowly began to wane.
But back inside my head it lurked,
Would I go insane?

Would I pass it on,
To the two whom I loved?
Could there be no release,
From below, beside, above?

There is no curse or it's reversed;
I have none to pass.
A joy in life, a love of truth,
To this my heart is cast.

Wholeness has emerged,
Though it was never free.
I paid the price of radical change.
The hard won prize — was ME.

MY EPITAPH

May I be known as daring,
Though mountains I have not climbed.
May I be known as an adventurer,
Though fame is not mine.

I've been brought to dare,
Cross into the unknown.
Leave the familiar
To myself atone.

Inside my mind,
Of strong feelings and pain,
Was shown stones in the water,
Each step to keep me sane.

The journey seemed impossible;
Inch by inch I moved.
Terrified, trembling, crying in fright,
Though given gifts to soothe.

Have emerged from horror,
To find a degree of peace.
Laughter, dances beneath the stars,
Joy of great release.

Most do not know,
The Great Escape I made.
I now know the joy,
As a wreath of honor is laid.

LIFE

We are all ordinary,

Doing as we live.

Hopes, dreams, connections,

As the moment gives.

We are here then gone.

Did we leave a mark?

Honor each and every one,

In the light, in the dark.

OPEN

A flower closes for the night,

Awaiting a touch of the sun.

I will help myself open up

With laughter's kiss of fun.

RUDE

I was so rude, so cutting,
Telling her, she did not know.
Wrong to think the thoughts she had,
Either fast or slow.

"Don't take your turn, ignore yourself.
Others know what's good.
Remember how others feel,
Worship the almighty should."

Laid on her a burden,
Heavy and so mean.
There was no hope for her,
None that could be seen.

She finally said, "I've had enough
Of your cruel, cruel ways."
Began to change her attitudes.
Follow wholeness many days.

She stood upright in dignity,
No longer would bend down.
Put my arms around her,
Loved her without a sound.

We cherish each other,
If the truth be told.
It is myself I cherish,
To have and to hold.

FREEDOM

Freedom

Not a gift from others,

But from yourself.

All too often,

Unwillingly received.

HATS

Wearing hats,

Not just for dress,

But for pride and all the rest.

Bold, brave,

Am I that?

When I wear my big black hat?

CLOSE / OPEN

Shut my mouth.

Shut my eyes.

I helped in making lies.

Didn't want to grow up.

Silly to see,

A 50-year-old child who was me.

I can think.

I can speak.

Now I dance upon my feet.

AWAKENING

Under the ground and far away,

Thought it was safe for me to stay.

Comfort some within those walls,

Hoped no trips, no chasms, or falls.

Why now a change, an opening I see.

Light entering and welcoming me.

Slowly I took some steps,

Beyond the wall where I was kept.

Fears and beliefs often wrong.

I did not know I could be strong.

CHOICES

He came himself to share.

With pain and joy I changed.

Took him in and found myself,

Far better,

When rearranged.

MY PAINTING

Had a little problem,

Burned a bridge or two.

Confusion in my mind,

No painting could I do.

Tried to build a bridge,

Using twine and tape.

No bridge appeared, to my surprise,

It led toward a gate.

Slowly opening it,

Came my friend and muse.

My art itself opened me;

Found the step to choose.

WHAT I SEE

Embarrassment,

Shame,

Circling in my cup.

Suddenly,

It hit me.

Do, lighten up.

THE GIFT

What could I give him?

What price will it be?

Chose the best.

The gift is...

ME!

ORDINARY

I am as ordinary
As I can be.
If you look for me
You won't even see.

A woman pulling weeds,
Admiring a thick, tall tree,
Eating a ripe dark cherry,
Drinking mango tea.

Caring for some,
Others left alone.
Spreading flame red paint,
In thick, juicy tones.

Looking for the dipper,
Guided by a star.
My human dust will travel
Far out to Mars.

ANOTHER LOOK

I saw myself reflected in others' eyes so wide.

Would I be judged as worthy?

Should I go and hide?

I made myself invisible so I could hide the pain.

Walking slowly, always looking,

For the Yellow Brick Lane.

I found a brain, courage to be.

Best of all found my heart

That is what I see.

B E

What a relief,

To stop and be.

Surrender pain,

I feel free.

INSPIRATION

His spirit inspires.

Though he's gone away.

Compassion, self-care,

Strong forces do stay.

Burn off the dross

By choosing to be

A powerful truth,

That is deeply me.

AWAY

It went away on the sly.

Don't know how or when.

It was with me, so very close,

As near as my own skin.

What did I do? What changed my mind?

No one is to blame.

Woke up one morning, it was gone,

The dark, dark cloud of shame.

PHYSICS

I am a connector — a conduit.

Realized I could send energy,

Light up someone so they sparkle.

Find they are Divinity, too.

THE WALL

Built a wall around me,

With bricks named fear and dread.

Old ideas held so close,

With those, my mind was fed.

A volcano has erupted.

Caused a shocking breach.

Light seemed far away,

Yet within my reach.

The light named "Change,"

Melted the wall where I hid.

Fear's seductive wail,

I will no longer bid.

STRONG

Being vulnerable

Is my strength.

I can bear the call.

Standing up,

Sip from my cup,

Truth prevents my fall.

F U N

I've had more fun under the sun,

Than many a person could see.

For I've learned to surrender,

That which is not mine.

Found I could really just…

Be.

NEW OUTFIT

Tried to fit the coat on,

Made of "bravery" and "risk."

He lent it for a while,

Excitement, fear well mixed.

It did its work,

One arm first, then two.

Buttons closed at last,

Strange it is, yet true.

N O

A woman's heart I did ignore,

Wanted to say, "nevermore."

But when he called my name,

I slowly came.

Out of the darkness,

Never the same.

THE ADVENTURE

Tiptoed to see a better view.

Looked far as I could

Tempted to enter in,

Decided that I should.

The view beckoned me;

Wild animals, vines so deep.

Walked right in, stayed a while.

Caution I did not keep.

Oh, the adventure there,

Would not tell a soul.

Will keep them to myself,

Within my heart enfold.

TAPESTRY

Wearing threads of life,

With uneven strands.

A human cloth I will wear,

Created by life's own hand.

ANCESTORS

Ancestors live in my core,

Telling of strengths, survival, and more.

Do not know all their names.

None of them had any fame.

Thanks for being, otherwise, I wouldn't be,

Rogues, saints, led to me.

BEING GROUNDED

Grounded, sounded

Boring, dull, brown.

Grounded revealed

Earthly joys found.

PHOENIX

There is a core, strong and deep

Within myself,

That does not sleep.

Risk, dare, try again.

Bloody, exciting,

Weave and blend.

Phoenix arising to be

A powerful force

Living in me.

Put it on canvas,

This I can.

It is myself, who I am.

I A M

I am as free as I let myself be.

I am as connected to others as I choose to be.

I am a partner with my Creator.

Not equal, but essential.

ANOTHER WAY

He didn't meet my assumptions.

He went another way.

He was not wrong,

But I was strong.

Lessons learned today.

POSSIBILITIES

What I need is laughter.

Myself — no bullseye.

Open up,

Take a step.

Could I possibly fly?

MINUS

I'm at a new normal,

Minus men, two and three.

Lost ten pounds in the process.

Size fourteen jeans, right for me.

AWKWARD AGE

I'm at an awkward age.

Not sure who I should be.

Trying different things.

Some things work, some things don't.

It's hard being 83.

STRUT

Get used to change,

Used to the unknown.

Think I'm crazy or what?

Sameness comes,

Not much fun.

Want to strut my stuff.

ARTIST

Decided to paint myself,

Using me, not a brush.

Vermilion, coral, aqua,

Black included — a must.

What colors will I use today,

On this canvas alive?

Spirit, direct my hand and heart.

I know,

A rainbow in the sky.

PERSEVERANCE

May I be a Siberian pony,

Sturdy against the wind.

Cold does not deter me,

Each day I begin again.

WORDS

Words help me heal,

Show what is real.

Not fancy to distract,

Sparse truth brings me back.

STAR

He was a booster rocket.

He carried me so far.

Finished his job,

Fell away.

I became

A star.

CHRISTMAS DAY

Dial it down,

Do not rush.

Savor the quiet,

So thick you can touch.

I'm not alone,

Though I be just one.

Warmth filling myself,

Might equal the sun.

NAKED

I am more naked in the truth I tell

Than any skin I show.

Revealing who I am,

Will I be received?

I risk all that they might know.

LETTING GO

Paired it down,

Just a few lines.

Sparse as sparse could be.

No clutter, no frills

To cloud the way.

What was left... was me.

DETERMINATION

Got a lot of nerve,

To ask for what I want.

Wise, safe, and sexy,

Two came, but left — a bunt.

You created me with nerve,

So you shouldn't be surprised.

If I ask for what I want,

See it with my own two eyes.

THE QUESTION

Someone asked,

What lay ahead this summer?

Things I'd do or say.

Been to Paris, Rome already.

Wasn't headed again that way.

Thought a moment.

Gave a "golden key."

Answered simply,

"I'm where I belong,

The place I should be."

LEAF

Painted a single gingko leaf,

On a canvas black.

Lines, shading showed me,

Something I had lacked.

Peace radiated from the leaf

Of the oldest tree.

Coming from deep inside,

It told of peace in me.

PICTURES

Painting pictures dark and grim,

Decided to show the mood I'm in.

"Are you always so happy?" someone asked of me.

"Take a look, tell me what you see?"

Shadow side within us all,

Can I be strong and bear the call?

Shadow side within each one,

Toward the truth, I dare to come.

CAFE

I thought I would be punished for having so much fun.
It seemed so irresponsible to take off on the run.
To drive and see a play that was truly confusing.
To walk outside, see the shops, the people all amusing.

No one to please, no one to chide,
I could risk it all.
To fail or to succeed,
I could bear the call.

Sitting with myself
To sip a glass of wine.
I could have good company.
It was truly mine.

I could savor actors,
Food taken from the shelf.
Best of all to savor,
Was really my own self.

LET GO

Holding on to unhealthy things;

Why do I do what I do?

Time gives space,

For my mind to erase;

Desires and wants,

Now few.

MY WRITINGS

One of the gifts of this time

Feelings deep, feelings raw.

No judging, but permission

For poems to tell it all.

TOWER

Painted a tottering tower,

Shapes ready to fall.

Triangles, squares unstable

What will be my call?

"Please stay up," I begged the shapes.

Now what will I do?

Voices answered loud and clear,

You will be made anew.

HEROES

See true heroes stepping up

Workers of all kind.

Leaders stand up to tell the truth.

See acts of love sublime.

Keep this human care

As we do move on.

Bring mercy, justice back

Which I feared had gone.

ART

Waiting is an art.

Thought art was paint and brush.

Can hear the longings of my heart,

When I stopped my rush.

HUMAN

Twisting, turning, up and down,

Calm and then some strife.

Expand, contract, risk, and pause.

All...

A human life.

NEW ATTITUDE

Being open is something new

Stepping in life's flow.

Not knowing what will happen

I pause,

Then...

I go.

OLD

Putting patches on frayed parts,

Sewing a rip or tear,

Washing out a stubborn spot.

It's myself, for which I care.

BOTH/AND

I embrace paradox

A key to modernity.

What is small, can be big.

A moment is eternity.

How boring it would be

Knowing the future for sanity.

Risks, though small, remind us all

Of our real humanity.

F O U N D

I've been foolish

I've been wrong.

What I found

I am strong.

AFFIRMING

I am somebody.

Not sure others know.

At this time, I take small steps

Living highs and lows.

Sometimes it's good to be

Invisible in the day.

Though I long for connection strong,

"You are somebody," they will say.

SHADOW SIDE

Scared to death of my shadow.

Want to see it erased.

Now, I know my shadow

Belongs in my warm embrace.

CARE

Who will take care of me?

Will there be none, or possibly three?

When I need care,

Will someone be there?

Spirit who loves us all,

Catch me before I fall.

Hold me in your arms so tight.

Save me from fear's dark night.

Live in the moment,

Was told loud and clear,

NOW is the time.

The moment right here.

NO TALKING

At first,

I did not know

I could speak

Long ago.

LAUGHING AT MYSELF

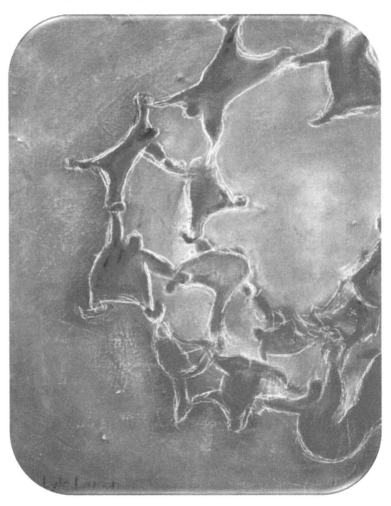

F U N

SHOE

Living in the moment

Is very hard to do.

Like fitting my head

Into a small, black shoe.

Don't focus backward.

Don't focus far ahead.

Must stay in the moment,

And try to save my head.

WARNING

A salesman came

To sell some gold.

A hapless buyer

Fell in the hole.

Beware what shines

Too good to be true.

The next buyer,

Just might be you.

SWEET

Just don't call me sweet.
Let me emphatically repeat.

I like to swear,
Go with uncombed hair.
Tell the truth when stepped upon,
Set boundaries from dusk to dawn.

Warrior woman, never give up,
Tell the truth in love.
Going through hell, emerging new,
Let all that sweetness shove.

Sugar candy on a stick,
Lollypops, chocolate for a mix.
So sweet for all to see, but
Definitely, emphatically, NO not me.

GOOD RESULT

I've always loved a garden,

Its scents and many hues.

I've felt a kinship real with earth.

Something I don't want to lose.

So when God calls me home,

I'll salute and say, "Aye, aye Sir."

Have my ashes scattered,

And make damn good fertilizer.

VISIONARY

Wait another 30 years,

For a vision led.

If it took that long,

I'd sing a song,

Then, be really dead.

MY CAT

Not to do,

Just to be.

Zen master shows me that.

Take afternoon naps,

Stretch as far as you can;

Zen master — my cat.

PARADOX

No wonder my discomfort

Am in a paradox.

Letting go, taking in,

Over the fence backward,

Jumped the fox.

My strong feelings are opposites.

Thought they should complement.

Have to try to calm me down.

Want to be upright,

Not bent.

HEAVEN

I've been thinking about heaven,

Here's what I hope...

You remember everyone's name,

Have whole bars of soap.

You find lost socks,

Don't trip and fall,

Hug loved ones,

Not hurt at all.

A PUZZLE

Not to be wasted.

Expands or contracts.

Can rush or linger fine.

It's hated or loved,

But doesn't care.

For me, its name is T I M E.

COMFORT

Buttered toast soothes me most,

Its grains moistened fine.

Life is good, for in this moment

Taste and comfort are mine.

ZAPPED

Want to be zapped by the Spirit,

Given a vision or two.

Glow in the dark,

But should I start?

Get dressed?

Brush my hair?

Yes, these two.

NEW MOON

Who hung that golden orb

Teasing me to reach and touch?

The clock stops its moving hands;

I'm lost in that celestial dust.

CHOCOLATE CAKE

One piece

Perfection

Whole cake

Addiction

CLOTHES

Got to get going.

What shall I wear?

The clothes I want,

Need washing with care.

Who would notice?

Soiled without a doubt.

Dusted them off;

Now, out and about.

MY OLD FRIEND SUSIE

Where oh where is Susie?

She disappeared not long ago.

It got cold, she got bold.

Put blankets on —

Her body warm below.

Hard to turn for comfort,

Tangled by sheets and fleece.

Cried, "I'm being eaten!"

Her house, I'm told,

Now, up for lease.

MACHINES

Thought machines complicated.

That is what I see.

Needed fixing,

What I learned,

Needed a different me.

SPELLING

Bought some time.

Didn't know I could.

Thought it had to pass.

Brought it home,

Watched it grow —

Changed spelling to thyme at last.

CHEF

Like to fall in love with a chef

Who'd gladly cook for free...

Delectable treats, I'd like to eat

With passion enough for me.

PURSE

Had a talk with myself.

Was very, very terse.

Why won't I put my billfold back,

In its section of my purse?

M E

Am going to fire my secretary.

Her filing just won't fly.

Though she knows the alphabet,

Can't find "F" or "I."

Told her so many times,

What I do expect.

She tries and sighs, but to my eyes,

She is derelict.

T. V.

Drug of choice,

No thoughts,

No feelings,

Sounds and images,

Keeping us numb.

MISDIRECTION

As I put on my "rag,"

Where is the tag?

Can't tell the front from the back.

Doing my best,

Slowly get dressed.

It's clear direction I lack.

BIG

Pillow at my back

Takes up some slack,

My big butt creates.

I'd need no help,

If I ate kelp;

But a big hamburger ate.

THE ARTS

Thanks for the arts,

Which energize my heart.

Makes me want to dance.

Even though,

I can't.

A FEELING

Feeling lighter

Sounds so sappy.

I found out that

I was happy.

DRINK

I'm going to get up,

Drink from my cup.

Wonder what's swirling around.

Look and see if I can tell;

Oh my God, one brain just found.

LITE POETRY

I love to make lists of jobs to do.

The longer the list, the better.

I cross them off one at a time,

From "getting out of the chair,"

To "washing my sweater."

I cheat and add a few things

Before the list was made.

Love to draw a line,

Through those words, quiet and staid.

In a world of unfinished tasks

Where uncertainty is the norm.

I finally see some progress,

Shining clear in the eye of the storm.

HUMMMMM

I've got to be a person;

Make some sense today.

Get things done, not much fun;

A straight and narrow way.

Looks alright, at first sight,

But kind of boring be.

Think I'll grab a neighbor's cat

And climb the nearest tree.

MANURE

Started the day resentful;

Told truth as best I could.

Finally, with a shovel

Did yard work as I should.

Thought I'd take a break,

But manure lured me on.

Put it on the bald spots...

Not my head, my lawn.

HELLO

No saint or sinner, that I am,

Just human through and through.

Urges, surges, real upfront,

Ready to meet you.

GROWING

This growing up bit

Is highly overrated.

Want to grow down sometime,

With chocolate sated.

BATE

Fished with bait,

It was myself.

The line fell with a dunk.

Felt a tug,

Pulled it up,

Surprise!

I got a skunk.

A FIND

Pin lost to wind my watch.

Was it a celestial sign?

Found it laying on the floor.

Now, I can tell time.

DELICIOUS

Have you ever tasted sunshine?

A juicy orange will do.

Savor the taste,

Don't let it waste;

Indulge in a ray or two.

THE DEVIL

Played a game with the Devil,
Changed his cards on the sly.
He caught me at it,
With a twinkle in his eye.

"You won't win,
So don't even try.
I've cards up my sleeve,
To use by and by."

Sweat itched on my skin
As I stumbled to play.
What card shall I choose
To save my day?

Called forth my Spirit
To risk and to dare.
Lay down all my cards
Releasing my cares.

"I've won just by playing,
Did not run away.
I'm battered, not broken,
I'm here to stay."

"You're a worthy opponent
I'll give you that.
Want to stay a while,
Just chew the fat?"

"Thanks, but I'm going,
Got some people to see."
Felt my Spirit rising
Strongly in me.

Quick he was gone,
But I knew it then.
He would test me out.
He would come again.

LOOKING

Looking for people who inspire,

Finding them more and more.

Passion, caring, creative folk,

Come into my room with no floor.

EFFORT

Trying to do my best

Is a daunting task.

Put effort, thought into it,

Then fell upon my ass.

OPPOSITES

Sweet and sour

That's what I am.

It's all an opposite mix.

Spit me out.

Drink me deep.

What will be your fix?

LOST & FOUND

Didn't have a sense of humor

When I first got up.

Bumbled around with half-closed eyes,

Drank coffee from my cup.

Sat to write a poem,

Found to my surprise

Ironic humor from inside,

Appeared before my eyes.

MARINATE

Let me marinate in love with

Spices of care, insight, seeping in

Till I'm ripe for cooking.

What a dish!

LIFE

Life offers lessons learned

Often hard for me to take.

The lessons I like most of all

Offer me ice cream and cake.

STANDARDS

Are your standards getting lower

As you go through these days?

I tracked in some soil

On the floor it lay.

Stepped around the pieces

As I did some tasks.

"Will I be here forever?"

The dirt began to ask.

Finally swept it up

With an insect big and dark.

This is my housekeeping today,

I have made my mark.

STEP

One step at a time

Would a 1/2 step do?

You want what?

Please ask just a few.

I'm sitting disheveled

A small lump of clay.

Yet you stretch before me,

A gift of this day!